D1475157

Moments With Father

His hands are gentle with beast or child... —FRANCES FROST

Moments With Father

Warmhearted Writings

About the Joys of Having

And Being a Father

Edited by C. Merton Babcock

Illustrated With Photography

♕ HALLMARK EDITIONS

MOMENTS WITH FATHER

Through the eyes of the child shines the love of the father....

—MICHAELS

MY LITTLE CHILD

Say of him what you please, but I know my child's failings.

I do not love him because he is good, but because he is my little child.

How should you know how dear he can be when you try to weigh his merits against his faults?

When I must punish him, he becomes all the more a part of my being.

When I cause his tears to come, my heart weeps with him.

I alone have a right to blame and punish, for he only may chastise who loves.

Rabindranath Tagore

AMONG THE 2ND RATE
AND 3RD RATE CLASS

Lord Randolph, the father of Sir Winston Churchill, was a very busy man while the future prime minister was attending college and military school. While Winston was a student at Harrow and, later, a cadet at Sandhurst, his father exerted his parental authority by correspondence. The following exchange took place on the occasion of Winston's receiving academic honors at Sandhurst.

Winston to Lord Randolph

6 August [1893]   Schweizerhof Hotel
                                            Lucerne

Dear Papa,

I was so glad to be able to send you good news on Thursday. I did not expect that the list would be published so soon & was starting off in the train when Little congratulated me on getting in. I looked in the paper & found this to be true. Several boys I know very well have got in too.

At Dover I sent off a lot of telegrams, and on the boat I received one from Grandmamma telling me I had passed.

We had a very rough crossing & poor Jack was very sick....

9 August 1893   Kissingen

My dear Winston,

I am rather surprised at your tone of exultation over your inclusion in the Sandhurst list. There are two ways of winning an examination, one creditable the other the reverse. You have unfortunately chosen the latter method, and appear to be much pleased with your success.

The first extremely discreditable feature of your performance was missing the infantry, for in that failure is demonstrated beyond refutation your slovenly happy-go-lucky harum scarum style of work for which you have always been distinguished at your different schools. Never have I received a really good report of your conduct in your work from any master or tutor you had from time to time to do with. Always behind-hand, never advancing in your class, incessant complaints of total wants of application, and this character which was constant in yr reports has shown the natural results clearly in your last army examination.

With all the advantage you had, with all the abilities which you foolishly think yourself to possess & which some of your relations claim for you, with all the efforts that have been made to make your life easy & agreeable & your work neither oppressive or distasteful, this is the grand result that you come up among the 2nd & 3rd rate class who are only good for commissions in a cavalry regiment....

I shall leave you to depend on yourself giving you merely such assistance as may be necessary to permit of a respectable life. Because I am certain that if you cannot prevent yourself from leading the idle useless unprofitable life you have had during your schooldays & later months, you will become a mere social wastrel, one of the hundreds of the public school failures, and you will degenerate into a shabby, unhappy & futile existence. If that is so you will have to bear all the blame for such misfortune yourself....

... Your mother sends her love.

Your affte father
Randolph S.C.

THE FAMILY DINING TABLE

Theodore Roosevelt, Jr., speaking of his famous father, emphasized the vital importance of the dining table as a family institution.

One of the greatest institutions of the civilized world is the family dining table. Food is not all that can be got from it. When guests were with us there was no ban on the conversation of any one, no matter how small either the individual or the conversation might be, unless the child showed monopolistic tendencies....

Even when Father was President and overwhelmed with work, both he and Mother made a practice of breakfasting with us. This meant an earlier hour for them than would otherwise have been necessary, for we had to go to school. In both generations the table has been treated as a gathering place for the family. There has never been a question of the children being served separately in the nursery....

FATHER MEANT ALL
THAT WAS WONDERFUL

Cornelia Otis Skinner, famous actress, monologuist and writer, was the daughter of Cornelius Otis Skinner, after whom she was named. Her father's profession required him to be absent from his family all too frequently. In the following account, Miss Skinner tells how excited she was while waiting for the train on which her father was expected.

…As the train roared into view, I'd hold my breath for fear it wouldn't slow down. Then would come the moment of panic for fear he might not be on board, followed by a gulp of joy at the sight of him swinging down out of the last car I'd expected him to be on, and a catapulting of myself down the length of the platform to meet him with a wild hurtle and a hand eagerly extended for the present he invariably brought me. Father's presents were simple, but to me they were treasures of delight: little dolls dressed in European costume, Maillard's "Langues de chats" in blue boxes with kittens on the lids, books on the Little Black Sambo order. He once brought home a harmonica and another time a xylophone — objects of joy for me and torture for Mother, although she put up with them in her zeal for my culture, thinking they might awaken in me some musical talent….

10

Sunday meant a large midday meal. And to make it more festive, Father usually brought with him a bottle of claret, of which I would be given a little tumblerful carefully watered. The salad course was in the nature of a ceremony, as Father always mixed the dressing. I can't recall a single meal when he was home, even on occasions of formal dinner parties, when Father failed to mix the salad dressing, in a great wooden bowl, patinaed with countless rubbings of garlic, slatherings of the best Italian olive oil, and guiltless of the sacrilege of soap and water....

Evening supper was generally oyster stew, or Father's favorite after-the-show meal, a bowl of crackers and milk. Then, for a brief time, he'd read aloud from Grimm or Hans Andersen, and as I grew sleepy he'd lift me up and carry me piggyback up the steep cupboard staircase, tuck me into bed himself, and hear my prayers. Then he'd blow out the candle and say, "Good night, Person," and go back to Mother and the sweet-smelling fire, and I'd lie listening to the comforting drone of their voices while the sound of the scampering mice and the thudding apples ceased to hold any terror for me.

MINIATURE

My day-old son is plenty scrawny,
His mouth is wide with screams, or yawny,
His ears seem larger than he's needing,
His nose is flat, his chin's receding,
His skin is very, very red,
He has no hair upon his head,
And yet I'm proud as proud can be,
To hear you say he looks like me.

Richard Armour

He is the happiest, be he king or peasant, who finds peace
in his home.   —JOHANN WOLFGANG VON GOETHE

WOULD A CAPTAIN
DESERT HIS SINKING SHIP?

Arthur Marx, in Life With Groucho, *tells how the famous comedian risked his life rather than admit he was wrong when all the evidence was against him.*

Father would rather do anything than admit he's wrong — even if it means risking his life. I know of no better example than the time back in 1927 when his stubbornness was nearly responsible for wiping out the entire Marx family and a Swedish nurse named Sadie.

It was on the day we were bringing Mother, Miriam, and the nurse home from the hospital in New York City where Miriam was born.

Father, in his anxiety to get Miriam home safely, was driving very slowly and cautiously, even for him. And when we approached the railroad crossing in Great Neck, he slowed the Lincoln to such a snail's pace that it stalled — right on the tracks.

Father stepped on the starter several times, but the engine wouldn't respond. At that moment we heard the familiar tooting of a Long Island Railroad train approaching around the bend.

"The 3:02 is right on time," remarked Father, glancing calmly at his wrist watch.

"My baby!" screamed Mother. "Let's get out!"

"And leave a six-thousand-dollar car on the tracks?" replied Father. "Not I. These cars don't grow on trees, you know."

"I don't give a damn about the car," said Mother hysterically, as Father tried in vain to get the engine started.

"Well, I do," replied Father. "She's got a lot of miles in her yet. She just flooded, but I'll get her started. Just be calm, everybody — be calm!"

But nobody was calm, and he couldn't get the engine started. The train came in view, Mother grabbed Miriam from the arms of the nurse, alighted from the car and urged the rest of us to run for our lives. But Father remained at his post, refusing to be swayed by female hysterics.

As the train drew closer, Father suddenly shouted out the window, "Hey, Ruth — in case I get killed, the key to the vault is behind *The Works of Shakespeare* in my study!"

Mother shuddered and refused to look. Father was quite pale himself. He sat there, grimly trying the starter, and, out of the corner of his eye, watching the train come closer and closer.

I often wonder what would have happened if the train hadn't turned out to be a local that had already started to slow down for the Great Neck station before it rounded the bend. Fortunately, it was, and it came to a grinding halt just ten feet short of the Lincoln.

"Damn!" said Father, as we all piled back in the car. "Now I have to find a new hiding place for the vault key!"

EIGHT CHILDREN OUTNUMBERED BY TWO PARENTS

Sam Levenson, in his best-selling book Everything but Money, *tells of his father's views of a "parent-centered home."*

As long as Papa was at the head of the table we were made aware of the unity of body and soul. There were rituals surrounding the care and feeding of both. Papa would take a small piece of bread in his hand, say the blessing, sprinkle some salt on it, then chew it slowly, thoughtfully, gratefully. He would then turn to the family and give the signal for the beginning of the meal with the words "Eat and remember." Once again we had been reminded that man is not an unthinking animal, and home is not a stable — certainly not our home.

Friday night's dinner was a testimonial banquet to Papa. For that hour, at least, he was no longer the oppressed victim of the sweatshops, the harassed, frightened and unsuccessful breadwinner, but the master to whom all heads bowed and upon whom all honor was bestowed. He was our father, our teacher, our wise man, our elder statesman, our tribal leader....

Although there were eight of us children, we were outnumbered by two parents. Ours was a decidedly parent-centered home....

Papa frequently used the "when I was your age" technique. When he was a boy he was older and stronger and smarter than any of us. He was quite a prodigy, to judge by his alleged childhood achievements. When he was my age he had a wife and six children, supported his aged parents, and earned the equivalent of a hundred and fifty American dollars a week while starving in a damp cellar.

"When are you going to start acting like a man?" was Papa's eternal query, even to my sister....

The only experience our family ever had with summer camping happened this way. When my brother Albert was about eight he was selected from a group of poor neighborhood kids because he looked, as Mama said, "greener and yellower" than all the rest, to be sent to a farm in upstate New York for a month to see if some red and pink could be added to the yellow and green. After about two weeks Papa went up to see how Albert was doing. When we met the train the next night it was not Papa but Albert who stepped onto the platform.

"Albert! Where's Papa?"

"In the country. He said he needs the vacation more than I do, so he took the last two weeks."

AS FINE A DAD AS ANY BOY EVER HAD

Michigan poet Edgar A. Guest was sixteen years old when his father died. In this tribute, he tells of the powerful influence his father had on his own career.

The people to whom we owe the most never remind us of our debts. They send no bills and they demand no settlement....

Why do I write this? Because I am thinking of one of the greatest of my own debts—the one to my father.

Lately I have been going back through the incidents of my life, trying to itemize the account. He isn't here to help me now; he kept no ledger in his dealings with me; he asked no return on his investment. I demanded much of him and he gave it all without one murmur of complaint.

Daily the debt grew, without my knowing it. In the first place, I didn't understand the kind of business my father was conducting in my behalf. Boys never do. I didn't know the extent of my drawing account with him, nor how diligently he was laboring to make my path the smooth one it has been.

I knew he was as fine a dad as any boy ever had—kind, cheerful, humorous, hard-working and patient; severe at times over my indifferent effort and boyish carelessness, but severe always with a kindly purpose, and very proud of his children whenever they did anything which seemed worthy. What I didn't know until too late was the depth of his wisdom and the magnitude of his sacrifice.

I was sixteen years of age when my father died, in the summer of 1897. My mother tells me that in his youth his hair was jet black. "The color of a raven's wing" was her poetic description of it. I can remember him only with gray hair which changed rapidly to white.

That snow-white glory fascinated me. It seemed to me to be the most beautiful hair I had ever seen on a man. He used to laugh at my adoration of it; and when, in my boyish way, I asked what made it so white he gave always the same terse answer: "It just faded."

I know now, what I never guessed back then — that white hair was the badge of my father's struggle for us all. He had suffered much, borne privations himself; stood to reverses; seen failure come, through no fault of his own; and finally, leaving the land of his birth and the friends of his lifetime, had come to the United States to start life anew, that his children should have their chance.

He died in his fifty-seventh year, respected by all who knew him, in debt to no man, and unstained by any act of shame or dishonor.

He was always the example.   —WILL ROGERS, JR.

FATHER

My father's face is brown with sun,
His body is tall and limber.
His hands are gentle with beast or child
And strong as hardwood timber.

My father's eyes are the colors of sky,
Clear blue or gray as rain;
They change with the swinging change of days
While he watches the weather vane.

That galleon, golden upon our barn,
Veers with the world's four winds.
My father, his eyes on the vane, knows when
To fill our barley bins,

To stack our wood and pile our mows
With redtop and sweet tossed clover.
He captains our farm that rides the winds,
A keen-eyed brown earth-lover.

Frances Frost

21

HONOR KNOWS NO CLASS

Former President Harry Truman gained a great deal of notoriety for his outspoken defense of his daughter's vocal accomplishments. On one occasion, however, he turned the tables and reprimanded Margaret for overconfidence in her abilities. The following letter was written in 1952, after Margaret had spent a weekend in Washington.

January 18, 1952

Dear Margie:

It was a most happy week-end. It always is when you are with your Mommy and Daddy. Your Pop has been carefully watching the progress and change in his daughter, just as he watched it from five to fifteen. You've never had any advice from your Dad except in your interests. When you were anxious to be a singer at fifteen your Dad told you to be sure you had an education first. You took his advice. Now you're faced with a successful career. Be very careful that you remember your background and bringing up. I want you to succeed in whatever you undertake. To do that you must give it all you have. Keep your balance and display all the Truman-Wallace mulishness where right and wrong are in the balance. Right must always prevail. Do not let the glamor get you. There are decent, honorable people among the very rich, just as there are

among the very poor. Honor knows no class. It is just as great and as necessary at one end of the scale as at the other. No one can say which is the top....
Great men and women are assayed in future generations. Your Dad will never be reckoned among the great but you can be sure he did his level best and gave all he had to his country. There is an epitaph in Boothill Cemetery in Tombstone, Arizona, which reads, "Here lies Jack Williams; he done his damnedest." What more can a person do? I hope that will be yours and your Dad's epitaph.

Love,
Dad

A FATHER'S HAPPINESS

To show a child what has once delighted you, to find the child's delight added to your own, so that there is now a double delight seen in the glow of trust and affection, this is happiness.

J.B. Priestly

Bright clasp of her whole hand around my finger,
My daughter, as we walk together now. —STEPHEN SPENDER

AUTOMOBILE MECHANICS

Sometimes
　　I help my dad
　　Work on our automobile.
　　　　We unscrew
　　　　The radiator cap
　　　　　　And we let some water run —
　　　　　　Swish — from a hose
　　　　　　Into the tank.

And then we open up the hood
And feed in oil
From a can with a long spout.
And then we take a lot of rags
And clean all about.
　　We clean the top
　　And the doors
　　And the fenders and the wheels
　　And the windows and floors....
　　　　We work hard
　　　　My dad
　　　　And I.

　　　　　　Dorothy W. Baruch

WHAT TO TELL A CHILD
WHO ASKS "WHY?"

In his typically humorous fashion, Mark Twain commented on the importance of paternal discipline in rearing a child.

Nothing can be more fatal to your discipline than to allow your children to contradict you. If you happen to be betrayed into any misstatement or exaggeration in their presence, don't permit them to correct you. Right or wrong, you must obstinately insist on your own infallibility, and promptly suppress every symptom of puerile skepticism, with force if need be. The moment you permit them to doubt your unerring wisdom, you will begin to forfeit their respect and pander to their conceit...I vividly remember how my father who was one of the most rigid and successful of disciplinarians — quelled the aspiring egotism that prompted me to correct his careless remark (when he was reckoning a problem...) that five times twelve was sixty-two and a half. "So," said he, climbing over his spectacles and surveying me grimly, "ye think ye know more 'n yer father, hey? Come 'ere to me!" His invitation was too pressing to be declined, and for a few excruciating moments I reposed in bitter humiliation across his left knee, with my neck in the embrace of his left arm.

I didn't see him demonstrate his mathematical accuracy, with the palm of his right hand on the largest patch of my trousers, but I *felt* that the old man was right; and when, after completely eradicating my faith in the multiplication-table, he asked me how much five times twelve was, I insisted, with tears in my eyes, that it was sixty-two and a half. "That's right!" said he; "I'll larn ye to respect yer father, if I have to thrash ye twelve times a day. Now go 'n water them hosses, 'n be lively too!" The old gentleman didn't permit any respect for him to wane much until the inflammatory rheumatism disabled him; and even then he continued to inspire me with awe until I was thoroughly convinced that his disability was permanent.

...When you tell your child to do anything, and he stops to inquire why, it is advisable to kindly but firmly fetch him a rap across the ear to inform him "that's why!" He will soon get in the way of starting, with charming alacrity, at the word of command.

HONESTY IS THE BEST POLICY

Joe E. Brown, the famous comedian, early in his life knew the meaning of poverty. He also knew the meaning of kindness and warm devotion with which large families envelop their clan. In the following passage from Laughter Is a Wonderful Thing, *he tells how his father taught him the virtue of honesty.*

My earliest recollections of my father are of his activities at North Baltimore, where we moved when I was four or five. At that time he was clearing land on contract. It was hard work, for some of the Ohio land in those days still bore thick strands of timber and thicker underbrush.

Times were tough — tougher than usual, that is — for Mathias Brown and his big family in those days. There were five children by then, and I was in the middle. I remember especially how, one winter, we depended on Dad coming home every night with a rabbit. It was about the only meat we had that whole winter. I don't remember that I knew the taste of butter except only occasionally in some more prosperous neighbor's home....We used lard, spread on bread and sprinkled with a little salt, or, on rare treats, sprinkled with a little brown sugar....

Dad was a painter, and, in his way, an artist. He painted houses, barns, outhouses, but he took such pride in his work that his honesty was a kind of artistry. He had a talent for giving a full day's work, full value for whatever he was paid. We were on our way to the local ball park one Sunday morning when we passed a house he had painted a month before.

"Now, look at that!" he exclaimed, stopping suddenly to stare at the house. "How could I have overlooked that?"

I tugged at his coattail, impatient to get on to the park.

"Wait, son," he said. "There's a spot on Mrs. Forker's porch I didn't get. I must go back to the house and bring some paint."

"But Dad," I cried, "we'll miss the ball game!"

"The game can wait, son," he said. "Mrs. Forker paid me for painting her house."

That was all he said, or would say on the matter. I was a grown man before I realized examples such as this were the foundation for my own desire to give my best in every job.

MY GARDEN PLOT

Bronson Alcott, who has been called "the father of
Little Women," *spent a summer in England in*
1842. Here is one of the delightful letters he wrote
to his children.

For Louisa May Alcott,
   Elizabeth Sewall Alcott
     and
   Abba May Alcott
     Concordia Cottage — from their father,
         15 July, 1842.

My dear Girls:

I think of you all every day and desire to see you
all again: Anna with her beauty-loving eyes and
sweet visions of graceful motions, of golden hues
and all fair and mystic shows and shapes — Louisa
with her quick and ready services, her agile limbs
and boundless curiosity, her penetrating mind and
tear-shedding heart, alive to all moving, breathing
things — Elizabeth with her quiet-loving disposi-
tion and serene thoughts, her happy gentleness,
deep sentiment, self-centered in the depths of her
affections — and last, but yet dearest too in her joys
and impetuous griefs, the little Abba with her fast
falling footsteps, her sagacious eye and auburn
locks...and mother too, whose unsleeping love and

painstaking hands provide for your comforts and pleasant things and is your hope and stay and now more near and important to you while I am taken from your eyes. All and each of you I have in my mind: daily I see you in my thoughts and as I lay my head on my pillow at night or wake from sleep in the morning…nor can the tumbling waters hide my group of loves from my eyes: the little cottage there behind the Elm, the garden round, strawberry red or colored vines…or corn barn play house, or street or bridge or winding stream, or Anna or Louisa, their lessons loved (and learned by heart, not rote) and Lizzy too with little Ab in parlor, study, chamber, lawn, with needle, book or pen… and so you see, my gentle girls, I cannot leave you quite: though my body is far away my mind is near and all the while, I hear and see and touch and think and feel your very selves — the life that lives in all you are and say and do, the mind, the Heart, the Soul — the God that dwells in you. And now be loving little girls and grow more fair with every day and when I come to see my garden plot then shall my flowers scent the fields and I shall joy in every scent they lend, in every tint and form they wear. So now, my dears, adieu.

Let mother read this with you and talk long and sweetly with her about what is in it and then kiss her all and each other and then her all again for Father's sake.

I AM A MODEL FATHER-IN-LAW

Thomas Henry Huxley, famous nineteenth-century scientist, wrote to his son Harry on hearing that he had become engaged to be married.

Eastbourne, Jan. 30, 1890

You Dear Old Humbug of a Boy —

Here we have been mourning over the relapse of influenza, which alone, as we said, could have torn you from your duties, and all the while it was nothing but an attack of palpitation such as young people are liable to and seem none the worse for after all. We are as happy that you are happy as you can be yourself, though from your letter that seems to be saying a great deal. I am prepared to be the young lady's slave; pray tell her that I am a model father-in-law, with my love. (By the way, you might mention her name; it is a miserable detail, I know, but would be interesting)....

Ever your loving dad.
T.H. Huxley

What do I owe my father? Everything. —HENRY VAN DYKE

SOLILOQUY IN CIRCLES

Being a father
Is quite a bother.

You are free as air
With time to spare,

You're a fiscal rocket
With change in your pocket,

And then one morn
A child is born.

Your life has been runcible,
Irresponsible,

Like an arrow or javelin
You've been constantly travelin',

But mostly, I daresay,
Without a *chaise percée,*

To which by comparison
Nothing's embarison.

But all children matures,
Maybe even yours.

You improve them mentally
And straighten them dentally,

They grow tall as a lancer
And ask questions you can't answer,

And supply you with data
About how everybody else wears lipstick
  sooner and stays up later,

And if they are popular,
The phone they monopular.

They scorn the dominion
Of their parent's opinion,

They're no longer corralable
Once they find that you're fallible.

But after you've raised them
  and educated them and gowned them,
They just take their little fingers
  and wrap you around them.

Being a father
Is quite a bother,
But I like it, rather,

Ogden Nash

...The glow of trust and affection, this is happiness.

—J. B. PRIESTLY

TAKE ADVANTAGE
OF THE QUALITIES YOU HAVE

Joseph P. Kennedy, father of nine children, including the late President John Fitzgerald Kennedy and the late Robert Kennedy, had a theory that "there is no other success for a father and a mother except to feel that they have made some contribution to the development of their children." That this theory was a working philosophy is apparent from a letter the elder Kennedy wrote to his son Jack while the future president was still a youth.

Now, Jack, I don't want to give the impression that I am a nagger, for goodness knows that is the worst thing a parent can be. After long experience in sizing up people, I definitely know you have the goods, and you can go a long way. Now aren't you foolish not to get all there is out of what God has given you?

After all, I would be lacking even as a friend if I did not urge you to take advantage of the qualities you have. It is very difficult to make up fundamentals that you have neglected when you were very young, and that is why I am urging you to do the best you can. I am not expecting too much, and I will not be disappointed if you don't turn out to be a real genius, but I think you can be a really worthwhile citizen with good judgment and understanding.

IN THE TYPICALLY ZIEGFELDIAN
GRAND MANNER

Patricia Ziegfeld is the daughter of Florenz Zieg-
feld, Jr., of the Ziegfeld Follies, and of Billie Burke,
the famous Hollywood actress. Patricia was her
father's child, and in her book The Ziegfelds' Girl,
she tells of how her father purchased an island in
Canada, which he named "Billie Burke," and es-
tablished Camp Patricia as a place to entertain.

…Daddy's version of Walden-in-Canada included
a main house, a guest lodge, a dining room and
kitchen under their own separate roof, a storehouse,
a dormitory for the guides, and a house built especially for Mother, with its own boat landing.

All the buildings were constructed of local peeled
logs, very primitive-looking outside, but inside
there was plenty of luxury — Canadian-woods-type
luxury, but luxury nevertheless. There was a huge
bathroom where I kept tadpoles that leapt out of the
tub when they turned into frogs, and got stepped
on by Daddy in the dark, Simmons mattresses
on all the beds, tall wrought-iron candelabra in the
living-room, and a camp-wide Delco system….

It wasn't hard for guests to put on twelve — or
even fifteen or twenty pounds — at Camp Patricia.
The food was marvelous and everything swam in
butter, gravy, and thick, rich cream.

Daddy, who loved to cook, was in his element. His specialty was a complicated dish based on a huge panful of fried tomatoes mixed with a dozen eggs and combined with corn and baked beans. It sounds ghastly, but it was delicious. He was also great at quail broiled in butter and smothered with quince jelly, and at a salad dressing that he mixed with the dedicated air of a scientist and that involved hard-boiled eggs, wine vinegar, paprika, and some exotic herbs that had to be imported from a gourmet shop in Montreal.

The only thing Daddy disliked about cooking was the cleaning up afterwards. This he always avoided, and when he left a kitchen it looked as though some great natural disaster had taken place in it, on the order of a hurricane or a flood.

It usually took Daddy four or five days to simmer down and relax enough to cook when he got to camp. At the beginning he would be tense, jumpy, and tightly wound-up. Then, suddenly, he would turn into a prototype of a French-Canadian woodsman, talking in monosyllables, stalking through the woods as silent as a cat, and growing a beard. For the first week it drove him crazy, but he bore the itching manfully. Comments on the beard were unfailingly loud and uncomplimentary, but Daddy never shaved it off until the day we left for home.

YOU WILL BE TWENTY-ONE

At the time of the invasion of Sicily, during World War II, General Eisenhower's headquarters were in "a damp cubicle not bigger than ten feet by fourteen." At that time he wrote a birthday letter to his son, who was also serving his country in the armed services.

July 12, 1943

Dear Johnnie: This is written from my advanced C.P. during the early days of the Sicilian attack. The papers keep you fairly well informed of our operations, so you know that this whole force is hard at it again.

Strangely enough, for me personally, the beginning of one of these major pushes is a period of comparative inactivity, because there is so much waiting for reports, while I'm removed from my main headquarters where there is always something to keep one hustling.

The main purpose of this note is to wish you well on your birthday. You will be twenty-one — a voter if you were a civilian! I wish I could be there to shake you by the hand and say "Good luck!" As it is, this note will have to do, although possibly I'll get to send you a teletype, too.

You will note that the ink seems to sink into this paper. That is because of the dampness in this tunnel where my office is located. The weather outside is hot and dry. You may be sure I spend as little time as possible in this hole — but occasionally I have to have conferences, etc. here....

It's time to go see the Admiral. He's one of my best friends — and a great fighting man. Good luck, and again, congratulations.

Devotedly,
Dad

FATHER KNOWS BEST

My son is 7 years old. I am 54. It has taken me a great many years to reach that age. I am more respected in the community, I am stronger, I am more intelligent, and I think I am better than he is. I don't want to be a pal, I want to be a father.

Clifton Fadiman

ADVICE TO NEW FATHERS

Every new father-in-waiting provides additional fodder for the cartoonists' pens. Will Stanton, one of America's funniest writers and an old hand at the maternity ward game, tells his secrets for getting through the ordeal with as little pain as possible.

Looking at your new baby through a nursery window can be a trying experience. First of all, I think we should stop kidding ourselves and admit that no new baby is much to look at. You can't stare at him very many minutes without feeling foolish. But you feel guilty if you leave. After all, the nurse has picked him out and wheeled him over, and if you walk away after a couple of minutes, you know she's going to give you one of those reproachful what-kind-of-father-are-you? looks. The only thing you can do is window-shop. You walk along and look at other people's babies, and they come over and look at yours.

Probably the most appealing characteristics of babies are their small size and lack of hair. But for some dim reason, the most admired babies are the ones that are the biggest and have the most hair. But when you come down to it, fathering a big baby doesn't require any more talent than catching a big fish. Not as much, really.

Any baby over eight pounds is "certainly a big one, isn't he?" Between seven and eight pounds is "real nice sized." Under seven pounds the father doesn't say much and other people become very tactful. "Doctors these days don't want the babies so big. They used to be much bigger. Why, I remember when my cousin Wymer was born —" A maternity ward is the only place where total strangers will tell you how much their cousins weighed.

Being tactful about hair is tricky. You can say, confidentially, that you've always thought bald-headed babies were cuter, but it's best to check the father's hair first. If he is also bald, the remark loses much of its punch.

It's safest to be noncommittal. If the baby is sleeping, mention how good he is. If he's raising the roof, say he certainly has a set of lungs. Better to avoid the expression, "He's certainly all boy." At best it's meaningless, and at worst, if you've made an innocent mistake, the parents tend to get huffy.

A young father is easy to spot, but if you have a touch of gray, people are in doubt. They look at the baby, then at you, and they say, "This one's yours, is it?" When you say yes, they don't know what to say — they had been all set to tell you you didn't look old enough to be a grandfather.

Dr. Spock and other experts have offered a lot of advice to new fathers, but there's one thing all of them have neglected — the flask. This is no place to save money. During these times it will be your closest friend and companion, so get a good one. Mine is in a handsome leather carrying case with a shoulder strap. A fellow in the hospital elevator noticed it and asked what kind of camera I had. I told him a Schnapps.

A SPANKING FROM F.D.R.

Elliott Roosevelt, son of President Franklin D. Roosevelt, found that paternal spankings were not always painful. In an interview with Bela Kornitzer, he gave an example.

Father spanked us rarely, although we were a rowdy bunch and did everything in our power to provoke our parents. I remember when I did get punished. Mother used to take me to Father's study, sit me down, and say, "Franklin, this has gone far enough. You have to teach Elliott a lesson." After Mother left, Father would instruct me to yell while he beat the daylights out of his desk with a ruler. Soon Mother, hearing my anguished cries, would run back in, begging Father to stop.

...I'm proud as proud can be,
   To hear you say he looks like me. —RICHARD ARMOUR

A HOLLYWOOD STORY

Cecil B. De Mille, the famous Hollywood producer of some of America's best-loved films, testified that his father's religion was in large measure responsible for his own tremendous interest in biblical themes.

My father studied for the Episcopal ministry. In the 1870s he was a professor of English. He met my mother who was a teacher of English at Lockwood's Academy in Brooklyn. She told him that he would have a much larger congregation to which he could deliver his message if he turned to the theater instead of the church. In the church he might be able to speak to thousands. But through the theatre, his message could go out to hundreds of thousands. When I came along, the mantle fell upon my shoulders in a new form — the motion picture — and I was able to reach hundreds of millions....

My father used to read to us every night — a chapter of the Old Testament, and a chapter of the New Testament. The memory is very vivid even today, more than half a century later. We used to gather in the library after dinner....Father always sat in his big chair. The yellow light fell upon him and would light the semicircle sitting around him: my mother mending something; my grandmother sewing; my two aunts, Annie and Betty, knitting;

my uncle John, then only about seventeen; my brother Bill, and myself—the effect was really that of a great painting, the lighting that of a Rembrandt....

I can remember how deeply moved I was when my father read *Hereward the Wake* and *Hypatia.* There I really got my first idea of great drama. It was from him because, as I have said, he could read magnificently. He painted a great picture as he read, and the picture came to life before your eyes. Some of those pictures I brought to life again in later years. I have been able to recreate them on the screen....

Being a father / Is quite a bother, / But I like it, rather.

—OGDEN NASH

CASTOR OIL OR HONESTY

Fatherhood sometimes demands a little dishonesty. Frederic F. Van de Water, American writer and novelist, makes a confession to his grown son about his true feelings years earlier, when forced to administer castor oil.

The doctor had said that you must take it. I prepared the hideous draught as inoffensively as I could and I gagged while I did it. Thereafter came the ordeal of pouring it into you. After one taste, you shuddered and wept. The only difference in our reactions was that I did not weep.

Yet, obviously, sternness was my role. Your mother came to my aid. Together, at last, we got the ghastly mess inside you, but you gulped it down only after she had said:

"Come. Be a man. Would Daddy make all this fuss over nothing more than a little castor oil?"

I quailed even then, at the thought of the act Daddy would have staged if he had been you. You swallowed falsehood and oil together. If I had been honest, instead of a father, I should have told you while I held the cup to your lips:

"I don't blame you for yelling, kid. It would take seven large men to get such a hellish thing into me. Come now, be a good boy and drink it down."

That would have been the so-called enlightened

way for a parent to treat his son. Would you have taken the castor oil? You would not.

Since then, I have atoned at least in part for my dissembling. I have taken castor oil myself, not primarily because a doctor bade me, but to justify belatedly my stalwart pretense when I administered it to you.

FATHER SEWS ON A BUTTON

Clarence Day, in Life With Father, *relates the hilarious incident of the elder Day attempting to sew on a button.*

Mother felt that it was a woman's duty to mend things and sew, but she hated it....

Buttons were Father's worst trial, however, from his point of view. Ripped shirts and socks with holes in them could still be worn, but drawers with their buttons off couldn't. The speed with which he dressed seemed to discourage his buttons and make them desert Father's service. Furthermore, they always gave out suddenly and at the wrong moment.

He wanted help and he wanted it promptly at such times, of course. He would appear at Mother's door with a waistcoat in one hand and a disloyal button in the other, demanding that it be sewn on at once. If she said she couldn't just then, Father would get as indignant as though he had been drowning and a lifeguard had informed him he would save him tomorrow.

When his indignation mounted high enough to sweep aside his good judgment, he would say in a stern voice, "Very well, I'll sew it on myself," and demand a needle and thread....

Mother reluctantly gave these implements to him. He marched off, sat on the edge of his sofa in the middle of his bedroom, and got ready to work. The gaslight was better by his bureau, but he couldn't sit on a chair when he sewed. It had no extra room on it. He laid his scissors, the spool of thread, and his waistcoat down on the sofa beside him, wet his fingers, held the needle high up and well out in front, and began poking the thread at the eye.

Like every commander, Father expected instant obedience, and he wished to deal with trained troops. The contrariness of the needle and the limp obstinacy of the thread made him swear. He stuck the needle in the sofa while he wet his fingers and stiffened the thread again. When he came to take up his needle, it had disappeared. He felt around everywhere for it. He got up, holding fast to his thread, and turned around, facing the sofa to see where it was hiding. This jerked the spool off onto the floor, where it rolled away and unwound....

Father sewed on the button in a violent manner,

with vicious haulings and jabs. Mother said she couldn't bear to see him — but she couldn't bear to leave the room, either. She stood watching him, hypnotized and appalled, itching to sew it herself, and they talked at each other with vehemence. Then the inevitable accident happened: the needle came forcibly up through the waistcoat, it struck on the button, Father pushed at it harder, and it burst through the hole and stuck Father's finger.

He sprang up with a howl. To be impaled in this way was not only exasperating, it was an affront. He turned to me, as he strode about on the rug, holding onto his finger, and said wrathfully, "It was your mother."

"Why, Clare!" Mother cried.

"Talking every minute," Father shouted at her, "and distracting a man! How the devil can I sew on a button with this gibbering and buzz in my ears? Now see what you made me do!" he added suddenly. "Blood on my good waistcoat! Here! Take the damned thing. Give me a handkerchief to tie up my finger with. Where's the witch-hazel?"

THE EXAMPLE

He was always the example. In those days parents assumed an automatic leadership I don't see in parents today, including myself. My father was the head of the house. He behaved as the head of the house. He was the parent, kindly, generous, but definite. When he said it should be done, it was done. That fashioned us when we were young.

Will Rogers, Jr.

TO MY DAUGHTER

Bright clasp of her whole hand around my finger,
My daughter, as we walk together now.
All my life I'll feel a ring invisibly
Circle this bone with shining: when she is grown
Far from today as her eyes are far already.

Stephen Spender

THAT BOY IS GOING TO MAKE
A GREAT TRACK MAN

*Following the untimely death of Knute Rockne in
an airplane crash on March 31, 1931, his wife, Bon-
nie, published the famous coach's autobiography.
In her editorial note, she paid tribute to Knute as
an ideal father.*

No one who knew Knute — no one who ever heard
anyone speak intimately of him — could doubt that
he was a devoted home man....I do not see how any
husband or father could be nobler or kinder....

Knute was never happier than when sharing the
amusements, the games and the noisy delights of
our children. Indeed, he was always interested in
all little ones and always very kind to them. He
used to get a particular thrill, naturally, out of the
bright sayings of our own youngsters....He was
acutely interested in watching them develop in
anything they took up, but I have excellent reason
to suspect he had a particular delight in finding
them interested in athletic development....Once,
for instance, Junior was momentarily dedicated to
gentle discipline for some anti-social act, but the
agile Junior made such a speedy getaway that
Knute had to put on all his steam to catch him.
Paternal discipline mildly vindicated, Knute
brushed the perspiration from his brow and said

with a happy smile, "That boy is going to make a great track man!"...

Once Knute playfully demanded of one of the boys an account of his age. He answered, "Seven." "Impossible," his father said; "no young man could possibly get quite so dirty in seven years." Then he tried to placate the boy's mother with a grotesquely penitential look.

Sometimes his boys would get a good practical joke on their dad and almost perish of glee, but no one enjoyed the joke more than Knute.

Although widely and justly acclaimed for his stories, Knute seldom told them at home — except such amusing incidents of the day as delighted us all. His story telling was chiefly for public appearances when with his football friends, old college chums and favorite coaches and sports writers....

The children, of course, had their own special hour before they could be reconciled to sleep. At such times he recited nursery rhymes or told bear stories — not the athletic kind. Here is a sample of the bedside poetry!

> "There is a boarding-house far, far away
>   Where they serve ham and eggs three
>   times a day.
>   Woe, woe! the boarders yell
>   When they hear the dinner bell
>   For they know the eggs will smell far,
>   far away."

A father sees a son nearing manhood.
What shall he tell that son? —CARL SANDBURG

I HAVE A PICTURE IN MY MIND

Marian Anderson, the celebrated contralto, remembers her father for the joy he brought into the lives of his children. He died when his talented daughter was ten years old, but not before she had made her first public appearance. Following are some of Miss Anderson's reminiscences from her autobiography, My Lord, What a Morning.

I remember John Anderson, my father, very clearly. We do not have any photograph of him, but I have a picture in my mind of a man, dark, handsome, tall, and neither too stout nor too thin. I cannot say how tall, but he was well over six feet and stood very erect. Mother is a tiny woman; when she and I stand side by side, her head does not reach quite up to my shoulder. I remember once when she was helping Father put on his tie and she was reaching up on tiptoe. He laughed heartily and told her to get a newspaper to stand on to make herself a little taller.

I don't know all the things my father did to earn a living. As a child I was not concerned. But I do know that for many years he was employed by day at the Reading Terminal Market, in the refrigerator room, and we looked forward to his homecoming every evening. At the end of the week — not every week, of course — he would bring home a long, golden bar of pound cake, and my appetite for all other food would vanish. I am told that he sold coal and ice, and he had other jobs. I know he worked hard and looked after his family well....

Our big outing each year was a trip to the Barnum and Bailey Circus. To us it was like a great journey away from home. We prepared for the day long in advance; it was the next biggest day to Christmas. Father would buy us something new to wear. A basket or two was prepared, and off we went, taking a trolley car for what seemed like an endless ride. We had wonderful lunches and afternoon snacks. Our eyes were big with delight, trying to follow all the acts going on at the same time under the big tent....

There were sad things to come the year that I was ten. Father received an accidental blow on the head while at work and fell gravely ill. The doctor discovered later that he had a tumor. As Christmas approached he lay helpless in his bed....

And then, a short time later, Father died in our home on Colorado Street.

A FATHER SEES A SON
NEARING MANHOOD

Carl Sandburg, America's beloved poet of democracy, set forth in his book The People, Yes *some timely advice from a father to his son.*

A father sees a son nearing manhood.
What shall he tell that son?
"Life is hard; be steel; be a rock."
 And this might stand him for the storms
 and serve him for humdrum and monotony
 and guide him amid sudden betrayals
 and tighten him for slack moments.
"Life is a soft loam; be gentle; go easy."
 And this too might serve him.
 Brutes have been gentled where lashes failed.
 The growth of a frail flower in a path up
 has sometimes shattered and split a rock.
 A tough will counts. So does desire.
 So does a rich soft wanting.
 Without rich wanting nothing arrives.
 Tell him too much money has killed men
 and left them dead years before burial:
 the quest of lucre beyond a few easy needs
 has twisted good enough men
 sometimes into dry thwarted worms.
 Tell him time as a stuff can be wasted.
 Tell him to be a fool every so often

and to have no shame over having been a fool
yet learning something out of every folly
hoping to repeat none of the cheap follies
thus arriving at intimate understanding
of a world numbering many fools.
Tell him to be alone often and get at himself
and above all tell himself no lies about himself
whatever the white lies and protective fronts
he may use amongst other people.
Tell him solitude is creative if he is strong
and the final decisions are made in silent rooms.
Tell him to be different from other people
if it comes natural and easy being different.
Let him have lazy days seeking his deeper motives.
Let him seek deep for where his is a born natural.
    Then he may understand Shakespeare
    and the Wright brothers, Pasteur, Pavlov,
    Michael Faraday and free imaginations
bringing changes into a world resenting change.
    He will be lonely enough
    to have time for the work
    he knows as his own.

A SON'S DEBT

What do I owe my father? Everything. He was my best friend: a parent who knew how to be patient with an unruly child; a preacher of joyful faith, who practiced what he taught; a good companion in the woods and the library; a fearless man with a kind heart; a Christian without pretense or bigotry; a true American gentleman of the democratic type. Every day I give thanks for him.

Henry van Dyke

Set in Trump Medieval, a Venetian face
designed by Georg Trump, Munich.
Printed on Hallmark Crown Royale Book paper.
Designed by William M. Gilmore.